Fun and Easy
Drawing

Fun and Easy Drawing on the Farm

Rosa M. Curto

Enslow Elementary
an imprint of
Enslow Publishers, Inc.
40 Industrial Road
Box 398
Berkeley Heights, NJ 07922
USA

http://www.enslow.com

INTRODUCTION

If you visit a farm, you can see many basic shapes. This book shows you how shapes can help you draw different things. Just follow the steps and use your imagination.

You can use markers, colored pencils, crayons, or paint to draw.

You can draw these shapes flat or with volume. When you draw with volume, you can see more than one side of an object at the same time. It looks 3-D!

Look at the fences, the door, and the container. The colored drawings have volume.

SOME TIPS BEFORE
YOU START DRAWING:

- CHOOSE A QUIET AND
  WELL-LIT PLACE TO WORK.
- HAVE WHAT YOU NEED TO
  DRAW AT HAND.
- TAKE YOUR TIME.
- HAVE FUN!

HEN

1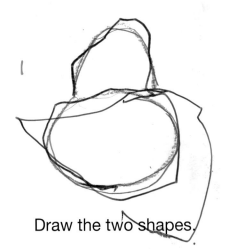

Draw the two shapes.

2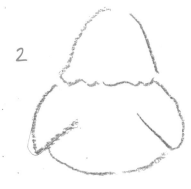

Draw the wings.

3

Draw the comb (red thing) on the top of the head. Shape the wings.

4

Draw the beak and the wattle (the red thing on its neck).

5

Color it in.

With some different lines, you can also draw a hen from the back.

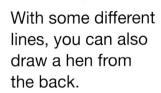

4

Follow these six steps to draw a hen standing up.

1

2

3

4

SOME TYPES OF CHICKENS LAY GREEN OR BLUE EGGS.

5

Add final details and color it in.

6

CHICKS

Draw two circles in different ways to make some chicks.

THERE ARE MORE CHICKENS THAN PEOPLE ON EARTH.

ROOSTER

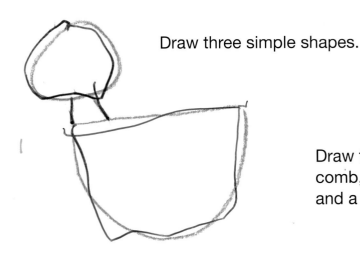

Draw three simple shapes.

Draw the beak, the comb, the wattle, and a wing.

Draw the legs and tail. Round them off.

Finish the details and color it in.

CHICKENS EAT SEEDS, GRAINS, FRUIT, AND BUGS.

GOOSE

You can draw the goose from two points of view.

Draw the first one from the side.

Draw two ovals and a line.

1

2

Finish the neck.

3

Add a beak and feet.

Finish the details and color it in.

4

1

2

3

Draw this goose from the front.
Follow the same steps as before.

4

LIKE CHICKENS,
GEESE ALSO HATCH
FROM EGGS.

TURKEY & PEACOCK

Start with two circles and a line connecting them.

1

2

Draw the neck.

3

Draw the beak, wings, and tail.

Add feet.

4

Finish it and color it in.

5

WILD TURKEYS CAN FLY.
FARM TURKEYS ARE TOO
BIG TO FLY!

1

2

3

You can draw a peacock
on your own. It is a lot
like drawing the turkey.

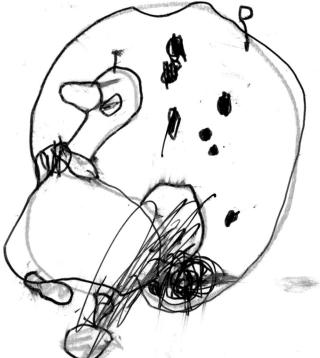

4

5

PEACOCKS ARE MALE.
FEMALES ARE CALLED PEAHENS.
ONLY MALES HAVE THE COLORFUL FEATHERS.

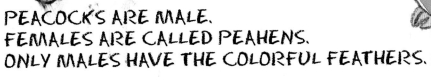

SHEEP

Follow the four steps to draw the sheep from the side.

1

2

3

4

SHEEP GIVE US WOOL.

Now draw a sheep from the front.

GOAT

Draw a triangle and rectangle for the head and body.

1

2

Add the horns and tail.

3

Round off the shapes.

4

Draw the ears and nose.

Shape the legs and draw the hooves.

Color it in.

5

A YOUNG GOAT IS CALLED A KID.

DOGS

You can draw these two dogs in three steps.

WHEN A DOG WAGS ITS TAIL, IT
MEANS THAT IT IS HAPPY.

Draw another dog in four steps.
Start with two simple shapes.

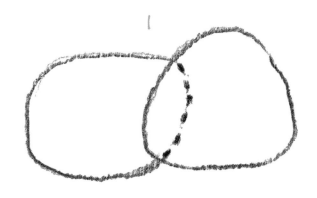

Draw the legs and tail.

Draw the nose and ears.
Finish the details.

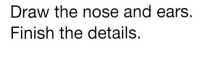

Color it in.

PIG

1

2

In four steps, you
can draw a little pig.

3

4

In three steps, you can
draw a pig from the back.

Draw another pig
in five steps.

1

2

3

4

5

SCIENTISTS BELIEVE THAT
PIGS ARE ONE OF THE
MOST INTELLIGENT
ANIMALS, RANKING CLOSE
BEHIND APES.

RABBITS

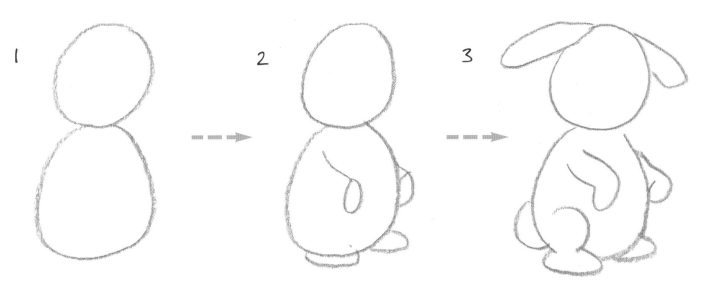

1 2 3

Draw a rabbit in three steps. Here is a rabbit with floppy ears.

If you want to draw a rabbit with ears that stand up straight, look at this other one.

You can also draw a rabbit
from the side in three steps.

1

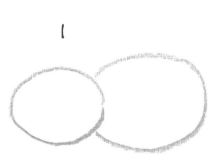

2

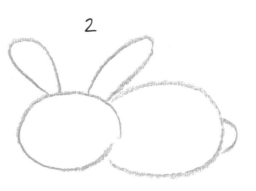

3

RABBITS WITH FLOPPY EARS ARE CALLED LOPS.

What do you think of this one
with an ear bent down?

HORSES

Draw three simple shapes and add the legs.

Give volume to the legs. Draw the ears and the tail.

Round it off.

Color it in.

Now, draw this horse in just three steps.

1

2

3

WHEN A HORSE'S EARS ARE STRAIGHT UP, IT MEANS THAT IT IS HAPPY. IF THE EARS ARE FLAT AGAINST THE HORSE'S HEAD, IT MEANS THAT THE HORSE IS ANGRY.

COW

First draw it from the front.

Then draw it from the back.

Now draw the cow from the side in five steps.

1

2

A COW CAN PRODUCE SIX TO SEVEN GALLONS OF MILK PER DAY.

3

4

COWS KEEP GRASS IN THEIR STOMACHS. LITTLE BY LITTLE, THEY BRING IT UP TO THEIR MOUTHS TO EAT IT.

5

Draw simple shapes.
Add his arms and legs.

Draw his overalls
and sleeves.

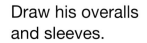

Draw his collar
and hands.

Give him some socks
and shoes.

Add a smiling face
and a straw hat.

Finish the details
and color him in.

**FARMERS HAVE TO MILK
THEIR COWS TWO OR THREE
TIMES A DAY.**

FARMER 2

Join three simple shapes together.
Draw her arms and legs.

Draw her dress and apron.

2

3

Draw a scarf on
her head and a basket
hanging from her arm.

Round off her arms.

4

Finish her legs,
socks, and shoes.

5

Finish the details
and color her in.

6

SOME FARMERS SELL
WHAT THEY GROW AT
FARMERS MARKETS.

TRUCK

Join two rectangles together.

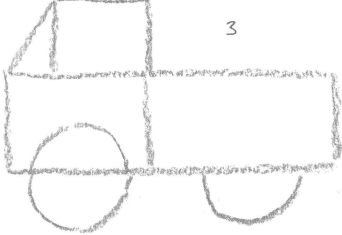

1

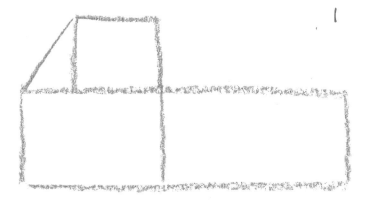

2

Draw a square and a triangle above the first rectangle.

3

Draw the wheels.

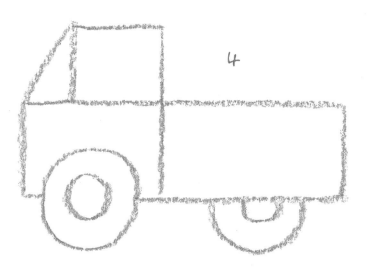

4

LOOK CAREFULLY!
One of the wheels is in front and the other is behind the truck.

28

5

Mark the wooden planks.

6

Add some details.

Color it in.

FARMERS DRIVE THEIR
TRUCKS TO THE
FARMERS MARKETS.

7

TRACTOR

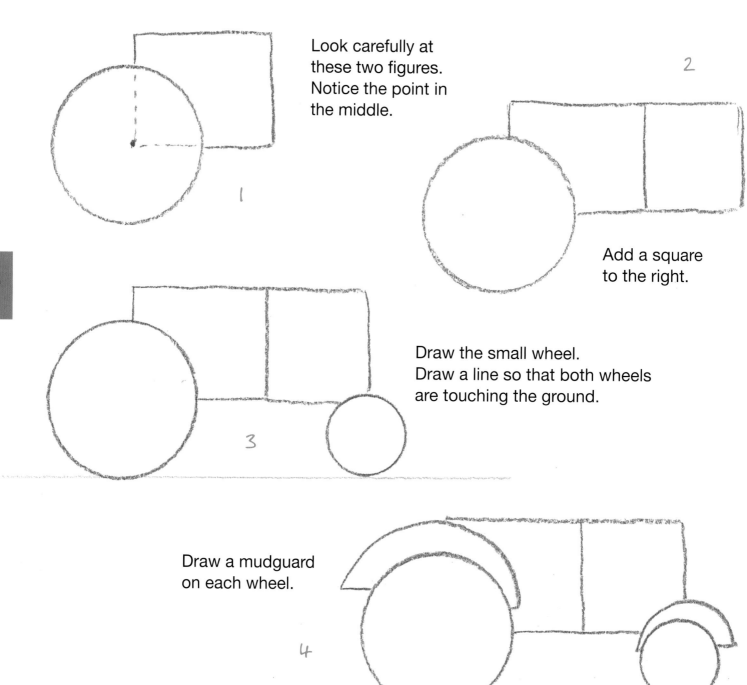

Look carefully at these two figures. Notice the point in the middle.

1

2

Add a square to the right.

Draw the small wheel. Draw a line so that both wheels are touching the ground.

3

Draw a mudguard on each wheel.

4

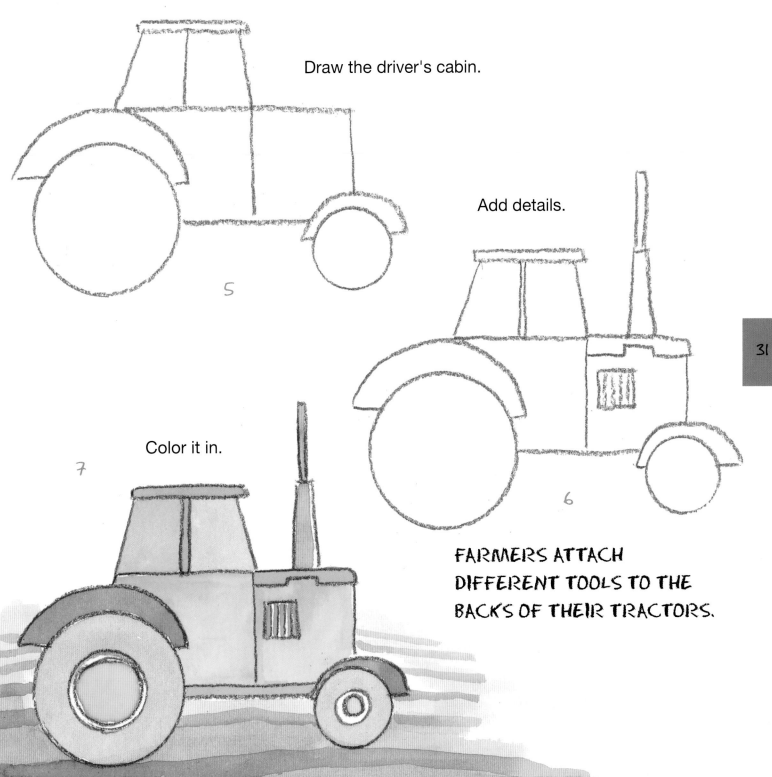

Draw the driver's cabin.

5

Add details.

6

Color it in.

7

FARMERS ATTACH
DIFFERENT TOOLS TO THE
BACKS OF THEIR TRACTORS.

THE DISTANCE BETWEEN LINES

Here are some simple facts that you will find very useful when you draw:

Look at this vegetable field. You can use lines to show distance. When things are far away, draw the lines closer together. The carrots will look smaller. When things are closer to you, draw the lines farther apart.

WHICH CARROTS ARE THE LARGEST, THE ONES AT THE FRONT OR THOSE AT THE BACK?

Now draw a road with trees along both sides. The trunks closer to you will be farther apart from one another.

THE TRUNKS THAT ARE FAR AWAY GET CLOSER AND CLOSER TOGETHER.

POINT OF VIEW

To create a sense of distance on a flat sheet of paper, you can use different points of view.

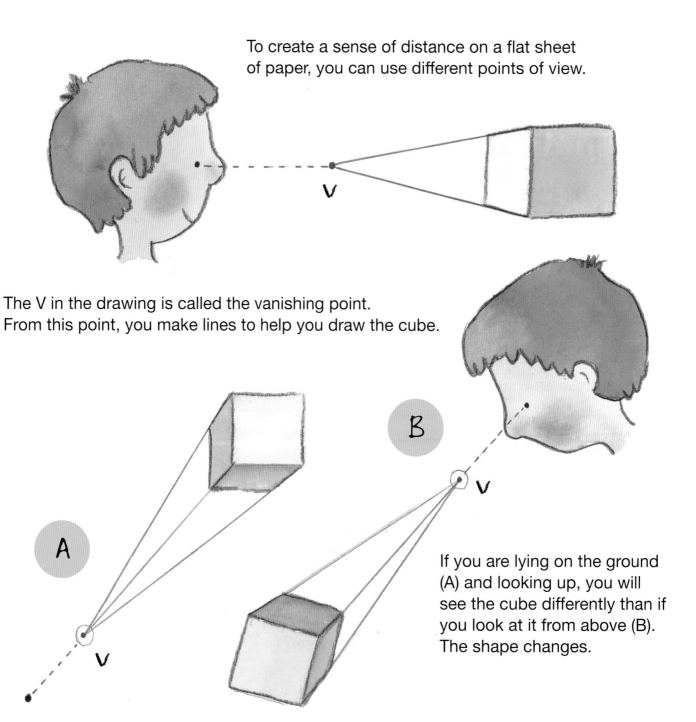

The V in the drawing is called the vanishing point. From this point, you make lines to help you draw the cube.

If you are lying on the ground (A) and looking up, you will see the cube differently than if you look at it from above (B). The shape changes.

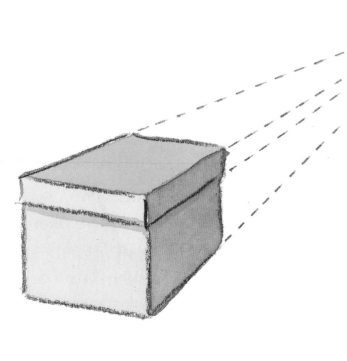

V

Here is a game for you!
Look at the box. There are some lines that end at the same point. This is the vanishing point (V).

Now copy these three boxes (yellow, blue, and red) on white paper. Lightly draw the lines that will help you find the vanishing point and mark it.

YOU HAVE FOUND THE VANISHING POINT THE OTHER WAY AROUND!

**REMEMBER:
LOOK CAREFULLY
AT THE THINGS
AROUND YOU.
IT WILL HELP YOU
LEARN TO DRAW.**

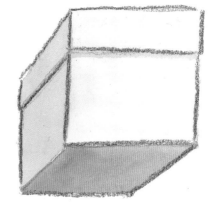

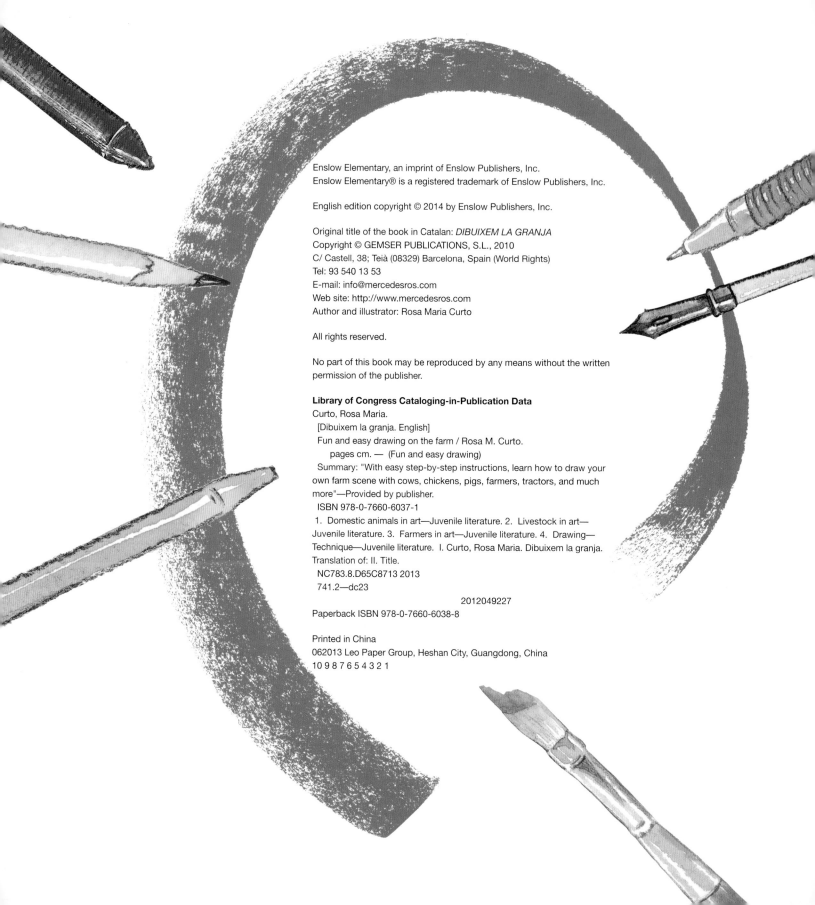

Enslow Elementary, an imprint of Enslow Publishers, Inc.
Enslow Elementary® is a registered trademark of Enslow Publishers, Inc.

English edition copyright © 2014 by Enslow Publishers, Inc.

Original title of the book in Catalan: *DIBUIXEM LA GRANJA*
Copyright © GEMSER PUBLICATIONS, S.L., 2010
C/ Castell, 38; Teià (08329) Barcelona, Spain (World Rights)
Tel: 93 540 13 53
E-mail: info@mercedesros.com
Web site: http://www.mercedesros.com
Author and illustrator: Rosa Maria Curto

Library of Congress Cataloging-in-Publication Data
Curto, Rosa Maria.
 [Dibuixem la granja. English]
 Fun and easy drawing on the farm / Rosa M. Curto.
    pages cm. — (Fun and easy drawing)
 Summary: "With easy step-by-step instructions, learn how to draw your own farm scene with cows, chickens, pigs, farmers, tractors, and much more"—Provided by publisher.
 ISBN 978-0-7660-6037-1
 1. Domestic animals in art—Juvenile literature. 2. Livestock in art—Juvenile literature. 3. Farmers in art—Juvenile literature. 4. Drawing—Technique—Juvenile literature. I. Curto, Rosa Maria. Dibuixem la granja. Translation of: II. Title.
 NC783.8.D65C8713 2013
 741.2—dc23
                                    2012049227
Paperback ISBN 978-0-7660-6038-8

Printed in China
062013 Leo Paper Group, Heshan City, Guangdong, China
10 9 8 7 6 5 4 3 2 1